Sohail Inayatullah

ANTICIPATION TO EMANCIPATION

Toward a Stage Theory of the Uses of the Future

The publication *Anticipation to Emancipation: Toward a Stage Theory of the Uses of the Future* was conceived with the support of UNESCO.

First edition, 2022

Series Editor: José Ramos
Production Editor & Editorial Designer: Abril Chimal
Illustrations: Charmine Sevil

ISBN: 978-0-6454283-1-5

Published by:
Tamkang University
Graduate Institute of Futures Studies,
Tamsui, Taipei, Taiwan 251.

About the Author

A political scientist and futurist, Sohail Inayatullah[1] is Professor at Tamkang University in Taipei. He is also a researcher at Metafuture.org, an international futures think-tank and an instructor at metafutureschool.org.

From 2016-2020, Professor Inayatullah was the UNESCO Chair in Futures Studies at USIM, Malaysia. He is now the UNESCO Chair in Futures Studies at the International Islamic University Malaysia. Earlier, in 2010, he was awarded the Laurel award for all-time best futurist by the Shaping Tomorrow Foresight Network. In March 2011, he was awarded an honorary doctorate by Universiti Sains Malaysia, Penang. He has lived in Islamabad, Pakistan; Bloomington, Indiana; Flushing, New York; Geneva, Switzerland; Kuala Lumpur, Malaysia; Honolulu, Hawaii; and Brisbane and Mooloolaba, Australia.

Professor Inayatullah received his doctorate from the University of Hawaii in 1990 and since 2001 has been the Editor-in-Chief of the Journal of Futures Studies. He has written more than 400 journal articles, book chapters, encyclopedia entries and magazine editorials. He has also written and co-edited twenty-five books and CDs. His latest (2018 in English, 2020 in Mandarin, and 2021 in Korean) book is Asia 2038: *Ten Disruptions That Change Everything and with Susann Roth, Futures thinking in Asia and the Pacific (2020).*

Abstract

Drawing on hundreds of case studies and decades of using the future in professional settings, this article moves toward a stage theory of the uses of the future. This deepens the Six Pillars framework and accompanying tools (scenarios, causal layered analysis, visioning) by inquiring which methods and tools are appropriate for which national, institutional, organizational and personal contexts. Seven stages are suggested. The first is perceived injustice - "it is not fair." The second is risk mitigation. The third is creating alternative futures. In this phase, the future is used to understand what happens if nothing changes, what happens if there is marginal change, what happens if there is adaptive change, and what happens when a different conceptualization of and access to power emerges. The fourth is directionality, the vision. The fifth is "making the vision real." The sixth is metaphor. In this phase, a narrative is created that helps move groups and individuals from the impossible to the powerful. The final state is personal and focused on using the mantra technique to transform the narrative. The entire process intends to enhance our ability to create justice in our perceived worlds, moving from one future to alternative futures, to the realization of preferred futures. The entire process is designed for the context of the user, to meet each person where she or he is at.[2]

Keywords

Futures Studies, Macrohistory, Foresight, Causal Layered Analysis (CLA), Scenarios, Metaphor, Mantra, Narrative Foresight, Futures Literacy, Transformative Change, Alternative Futures

Contents

Introduction:
A Castle Surrounded
by Hungry Wolves

I was presenting to over five hundred fifty plus mayors, councilors, policy analysts, and farming federation leaders at a conference on rural communities in regional Australia (Inayatullah, 2018). The Minister's staff had asked me to challenge their conceptions as to what the future could look like. During the presentation, there was a palpable sense of anger among participants. Many yelled out inappropriate comments. Most continued to drink alcohol. It was not just that they were exhausted from the day, but my comments only increased the challenges they had been experiencing. I suggested that the world would not get easier for them, but more difficult to manage. The audience tuned out, increasing their beverage intake. The Ministerial staff made a run for it, leaving me alone on the podium. While alcohol was a factor, it was not decisive. I had been ill-advised. I had given the wrong speech. I should have begun with their difficulties and found stories to reduce their pain, not enhance their challenges. In their life experience, the world was unfair; rural Australia was being decimated. Suicide was on the rise. Women and men were flocking to the major cities. They were in a middle of a cultural and population apocalypse. They did not wish for a new future, they wished for a different past. Or for reparations to be given to them because they were going through hardship, I had been unconscious of their context.

A second group - a Ministry of Education - wished for global innovation with the student at the center, taking classes from around the world, surrounded by ubiquitous technology and learning from whomever, wherever and whenever. But when we began to discuss the implementation of their vision, their anxiety grew for they sensed risk was everywhere. The underlying metaphor of their strategy was a castle surrounded by hungry wolves. While inside the castle, there was collegiality between the king, the queen, and the knights (the Minister, the Director-General, and the Principals), but outside the castle were forces of malevolence focused on retarding innovation.

A third group – a large steel company - found itself fractured. Some of the executives wished to create new futures, but the vast majority wanted to prevent a worse future - for them foresight was not about creating new opportunities, thinking differently, but about protecting what they had. It was the castle they loved - they needed futures thinking to help them buttress the ramparts not challenge their core global strategy. For those who wished to innovate, those in the castle were not just financially vested in the present, but their worldview had become a stranded asset.

A fourth group - a Ministry of Defense - when asked to envision a new health future instead wished for a rewritten past. They were traumatized from historical wounds, from loss of purpose in the wars they had fought. Listening to advances in genomics, virtual health apps, and nanotechnologies did not inspire, novelty would not bring back a lost past. It was a new narrative they needed that would help them journey to a new future, not fanciful discussions about what was next.

These and many other experiences have led me to reflect on the generic foresight processes futurists use to create alternative and preferred futures. What works best and when? Do individuals and organizations need to move through particular stages before they can create alternative and preferred futures?

Six Pillars
Straight Up

Futures thinking processes or workshop models have a clear pathway (Dator, 2002; Schultz, 2013; Voros, 2003). There is data input whether from the experts or citizens in the room or prior conducted scholarly literature reviews. Then the facilitator takes the group through several exercises to enhance their futures literacy. These are often methods such as the futures triangle, emerging issues analysis, the futures wheel, causal layered analysis (CLA), scenario development, visioning, scenario conflict resolution, and backcasting. From these methods, concrete outputs about alternative and preferred futures emerge. These could be a CLA to examine the issue, the organization today and tomorrow, or scenarios of possible futures. The output could be a preferred future with backcasting steps to realize the vision. There is often then an iterative process where the outputs become inputs for the next stage of the process, be it a strategic plan, action learning projects, or personal and collective insights for participants and others to reflect on.

In my work, I have used the six pillars process in workshops (2008; 2015). This process borrows extensively from the work of James Dator (2002), Elise Boulding (1995), Michel Foucault (1984), P.R. Sarkar (1984), Graham Molitor (2004), and Ivana Milojević (2005). The process is a structured, step-by-step use of the future to move an individual, an organization, an institution, a city, a country or a multi-lateral group from today to a set of tomorrows and preferred futures. It includes inner work on who the participants wish to become in their desired future and external work on the world they seek to create.

Pillar one is "mapping" with the core method: that of the futures triangle. Pillar two is "anticipation", with the core methods being emerging issues analysis and the futures wheel. Pillar three is "timing" with the core method macrohistory: in particular, the Sarkar game (Inayatullah, 2013). Pillar four is "deepening" with the core method CLA. Pillar five is "creating alternatives" with the core method scenario planning. Finally, the sixth pillar is "transforming" with backcasting and anticipatory action learning as the core methods.

However, in the past decade, workshop participants have repeatedly asked what are the most appropriate, the best methods for different situations. Do they need to go step-by-step through the six pillars (or other workshop models developed by luminaries such as James Dator (2002) or Riel Miller (2018)) or are certain methods more appropriate for certain groups or situations? This is has especially become urgent in the time of COVID-19 as workshops have been compressed from two to three days to a few hours per day at the most.

This is not merely a question of tailoring or focus, as every foresight practitioner does her best to ensure that the methods used address the research question asked. For example, when a CEO or board chair asks me to conduct a process, I always ask a number of questions. I generally ask: when individuals leave the room at the end of the day or days, what do you wish their emotional state to be? This is another way of asking for the product but focused on the inner level. Some state: "I want them excited about the possibility of a new future", "I want everyone aware of the challenges ahead." Directors also say - "I need to get them out of the day-to-day rut, they are too busy with what really does not matter." Or: "they see issues from only one view, I need to expand their worldview." "We have no direction or strategy - we need a way forward." "We understand that if we don't disrupt ourselves, others will disrupt us." These questions help me design the day, alerting me whether to focus on disruption and implications through emerging issues analysis and the futures wheel; deepening perspectives through causal layered analysis; creating a preferred future through visioning and backcasting; or reducing uncertainty through scenario planning.

A Stage Theory
Of the Uses of The Future

Based on these requests and attention to what works and what does not, I have developed the following step-by-step guide to using the future. It is a move towards a theory – or at the very least a conceptual framework - of using the future. This approach is insight and case study based. Unlike other research (Rohrbeck and Etingue, 2018; Chen and Hsu, 2020; Hoffman, 2019; Chen, 2019; Kelly, 2008; Pauw, 2018) I have few quantitative studies to "prove" the claims made below. Correlation and causation are implied, suggested, in the case studies but not proved (Inayatullah, 1991a; Inayatullah, 1990). There is a natural progression through states, however, and this is critical: hierarchy is not implied. Later stages are not better than earlier stages. We are all different: women and men have different contexts, as do those who live in the North and South, the city and village. Moreover, these are soft stages: one can move up and down as appropriate given the success or failure of the futures thinking/practice intervention. These stages are meant as assistive diagnostics so that the agency, capacity, and futures literacy of the individual or the organization can be enhanced.

The stage approach borrows from the work of P.R. Sarkar (1973) and his use of the South Asian system of kosas, wherein each layer of the mind takes us deeper. One needs to ensure that the body, for example, is well nourished through food before one can go deeper to intellect, and next to intuition, eventually leading to the stages of discrimination - what is of use and what is not - and enlightenment. I also borrow the framework from the works of Esther and Jerry Hicks (2004), who have developed an emotional scale of enlightenment, suggesting, for example, that the way out of depression is not a jump to bliss, as many argue, but anger. There are stages to move through before one can jump with joy at a future achieved. Sensitivity to the cognitive-emotional reality of the person/organization one is working with is crucial to success. The role of the futurist, the foresight practitioner, is to determine - given the worldview of those involved in the process- what is the most appropriate iteration of interventions. Once again, as futurists we need to meet the client/colleague/employer where they are at.

Stages
Social Injustice
Risk Mitigation
Alternative Fu-tures
Directionality
Making the Vision Real
Metaphor
Mantra

Stages of the Uses of the Future

Macrohistorian Ibn Khaldun reminds that all systems decline; thus, while the group may today be at the bottom, they may be on top later.

Social Injustice

In my work - and with a hundred plus colleagues[3] - I have noticed that stage one is the state of social injustice, the perception that reality is not fair. Individuals and collectivities are best served by a focus on theories of social change: particularly, thinkers that help them understand that their state is not eternal. Macrohistorian Ibn Khaldun reminds that all systems decline; thus, while the group may today be at the bottom, they may be on top later. Sorokin suggests that systems sway back and forth in a pendulum motion, between centralization and decentralization, for example, or between a concern for inclusion - soft solutions - to infrastructure planning, hard engineering solutions. One group of city planners that were focused on homelessness saw that their projects were about to be terminated since a new mayor, who was focused on tunnels and security, had been elected. The works of Sorokin helped them understand that they had to be patient - "hitting the wall with their heads" would not work, as the system was unlikely to budge. Insight and understanding are crucial here. Once this is understood - within the terms of the participants - then I try and move toward theories that create change. One can use Polak (1973) and move the system toward a perception that the future can be bright and that they can influence this future. One can use Toynbee (1972) and search for the creative minority. Or one can use Shrii Sarkar (1984) and help them understand that reality is cyclical, but through balanced leadership, a spiral can be created. Finally, Riane Eisler's (1987) macrohistorical template reminds about the possibilities of gender arrangements in terms of strict hierarchy (patriarchy) or more a more egalitarian one (the partnership model). Neither of these stages is fixed or given, and participants can investigate where their organisation or society is located. Scenarios that show macrohistorical patterns can be especially powerful.

With one community whose collective income, life opportunities, and health indicators were challenging to say the least, they articulated stage-like scenarios (Milojević and Inayatullah, 2018, p. 8). In the first scenario, present trends continue, and nothing is done. They called this scenario: "We die out." In the second, the status quo, they saw themselves as a "struggling snail." Marginalization continues with no effort to create new strategies. In the third, "our powers and numbers are increasing", health and employment conditions improve as the community becomes futures oriented. They use the future to start to transform the present. In the fourth scenario, employment and health are secondary to the primary issue of self-governance. This was the scenario of: "self-governance by Tjukurpa." The last scenario was the radical outlier - this was a world where community was first, place-land based spirituality was foundational, a universal basic income had been implemented, and it was indigenous peoples who had discovered the rest. Based on a short film this was called: Uber Babakiueria.

Indigenous Workforce Scenarios

Collapse	Status Quo	Marginal Change	Adaptive	Radical
Violence, unemployment, and substance abuse. School dropout rates increase. Rural areas continue to decline. Increased prison population.	Marginalized and disadvantaged. Aboriginal organisations overwhelmed. Not focused on jobs of the future.	More graduates, more Aboriginal people in higher paid positions, with clear career pathways.	Gaps in life outcomes are closed through greater full self-determination. Aboriginal organisations are the employers of choice. Health is prevention based.	Reversal in power with Aborigines in power. An Aboriginal Prime Minister. Society changes with a focus on community, country, cultural connection, and family relationships.
We die out	Struggling snail	Our numbers and powers are increasing?	People first – governed by Tjukulpa?	Uber Babakiueria

While the content is important in these scenarios, the real issue to note is that in each stage community power increases, reality becomes preferred. The narrative moves from the impossible to the powerful. The future is used to understand what happens if nothing changes, what happens if there is marginal change, and what begins to happen when power is applied and accessed differently.

In a group of students, we were working with after the violent break up of their nation, they were concerned that the workshop was moving too quickly toward the impossible vision. It was the worst case that first needed to be addressed. We thus first focused on what would happen if the trauma of the war continued. They excelled at this task, imagining physical violence moving to market violence (their local food supply chains being upended by fast food corporations). Once they felt heard, we could move toward the preferred future.

To move from this stage, four points are crucial: (1) Hearing and acknowledging the pain; (2) Using macrohistory to find theories of change that create a narrative that their time is to come; (3) Change what is within reach, within one zone of control; and (4) personalize the future. This is crucial so change does not become too grand of a project, it should be either personal or generational.

The main goal is to help groups and individuals empower themselves to enhance their ability to create justice in their perceived worlds.

" Understandably a focus on defending one's perspective comes first. One group suggested that the first response scenario was to kill the vegans, **the second to kill** the scientists, and the third to kill early adopters. "

Risk Mitigation

And if power has been achieved, then what? Many groups who have power wish to retain it, obviously. For them, foresight is about using the future to mitigate against external situations where profits, power, social capital - "the loot" - disappear. With this group, while certainly the big picture of macrohistory is important, they care little for grand patterns of change, for the longue durée; rather it is events and issues that could potentially disrupt their business model that are most important. Molitor's Emerging Issues Analysis is the most important method in this phase. The S-curve helps organizations understand that they are too focused on current problems and have not spent enough time identifying future risks. Once this is done, then the implications of these risks can be teased out with futures wheel. Following that, new areas of opportunity can be explored, helping the organization move from what it is good today to new capabilities for tomorrow. Often, I explore the structural implications of the vegan (Hancox, 2018) and plant-based revolution as well as the in vitro meat based revolution (cellular agriculture) (Ferguson and Colditz, 2019; Lamb, 2019). This challenges the worldviews of departments of agriculture and those in the food business. They can either see these new products and the cultural shift this is part of - new science, new tastes - as a threat or as an opportunity. Understandably a focus on defending one's perspective comes first. One group suggested that the first response scenario was to kill the vegans, the second to kill the scientists, and the third to kill early adopters. It is only with a great deal of effort that certain individuals begin to see that their core product - land, meat, milk, loans to the agricultural industry - may become a stranded asset (Macgeorge, 2019). General Electric (Sutherland, 2018) recently had that experience when their high performing assets - the fossil fuel industry - swiftly became stranded assets as individuals and nations move toward carbon neutral realities, as renewables become the likely future. Instead of defending the current reality, the used future - what worked before, but no longer does - it is more appropriate to look for new products and new markets - financial and epistemic. These could be a shift towards organics, or investments in cellular agriculture, or becoming hubs for "the new meat" in nearby regions (for example, just as in Islamic finance, where Malaysia and Singapore lead).

Creating the opportunity best comes from the futures wheel method. In a workshop organized by the South African government, we explored the pricing shift toward solar. Implications included the main energy company (ESKOM) disappearing, going bankrupt. Alternatively, it could purchase solar companies and retool. A third choice was not just to go solar nationally, but all over Africa - electrify the entire continent. Finally, one group of engineers suggested creating an "uber of energy" - each African village would use solar and then ESKOM would develop a peer-to-peer energy exchange scheme. This system would also challenge the gendered politics of energy ownership, as local grids would likely be managed by women. They would need to change who they were, who they hired, not just a retooling, but a transformation. This would be not just a change in technology, but in power. As it turns out for various political reasons, in particular the power of the nuclear lobby, this trajectory did not occur. Instead, it is in Bangladesh that the first peer to peer energy trading scheme has occurred (Peter, 2018). Challenging used futures - institutional practices that are no longer aligned to the vision of desired results - or stranded assets is not just a technical issue, but also a political issue. We have seen this with Grameen Bank, where a shift to decentralized energy practices led to female borrowers becoming empowered. Indeed, in a project with the Ministry of Health in Bangladesh, the used future was considered the current command/control hospital and city-centered health system. The preferred model would focus on "moving the data, not the patient", with local woman leaders conducting early health diagnostics. They would reduce personal health risks and the financial health risk to the country through preventive medicine (Sheraz, Inayatullah, and Shah, 2013).

With one large community organization focused on mental illness and health, it became clear that advances in artificial intelligence (AI) could be a great risk or an opportunity. The latter was possible if they could create partnerships between those with lived experience, community case workers, local city councils, law enforcement, and health professionals. If they did not, then AI could become one more oppressive force for those in mental anguish. To reduce risk and create opportunity, they suggested a narrative shift from "a world of roadblocks" to "creating the data tree." This entailed using AI to share real time data on illness and wellness to all stakeholders, creating a "Google" of health.

Similarly, in the disability field, participants at several futures workshops expressed how training carers who were technology savvy – interactive care - could be a pivotal factor in reducing the isolation experienced by persons with disability. Technology plus trained carers could be the opportunity; telecommunications technology alone – often slow, unreliable – could make conditions even worse.

To move out of this stage, it is crucial to acknowledge risk aversion, and then slowly shift toward possible opportunities. Data orientation, i.e., quantitative evidence to back up any possible futures, is critical as decision-makers will not support a project based on intuition or hunches. Examples or case studies of other nations, cities, organizations, and persons having used the future successfully are crucial for conceptual movement to occur.

Creating Alternatives

To enhance the possibility of moving from used or stranded futures to futures with opportunity, the possibility of change, the critical pathway is to move from one future to many futures. Individuals and organizations need to assess what the alternatives are before choices are made. Indeed, it is this notion of alternative futures that distinguishes Futures Studies from other disciplinary frames, as Magoroh Maruyama (1971), James Dator (2011) and Zia Sardar (2010) have argued. For example, in the earlier example on the rise of the new meat (as technology and as movement), should national governments defend their agricultural system? Should they innovate and become global players in the new system? Should they go even further and disrupt the new meat model (one group is even creating meat-based vegetables) with meat that looks like a vegetable? Or is the real issue, not so much about protein but about the supply chain - is the real disruption 3D printed food, where food as software is decisive? Or is the issue less about technology but about privilege? Is the first step to innovation ending the feudal landlord system in various nations? Flattening can be the necessary step so that innovation is adaptive and not merely technical.

Alternative futures thinking explores questions about the future not with the answer, but with a range of answers - each with different assumptions. The goal in this approach is to challenge assumptions, to ensure the scenarios developed are different from each other, not merely a variation of the initial assumption. For example, working with national governments on infrastructure planning, the issue moves from creating new roads to rethinking mobility. In one workshop in Singapore, the conversation moved from quicker roads to cars that were upwardly mobile - going up and down buildings - to drones, to using the rivers for transport, to finally a narrative wherein "everyone is within reach." Thus, the question moved from cars and transport to designing mobility in all systems. Alternative futures thinking thus rethinks the core assumptions we have of today. This creates a distance from the now, thus allowing new futures to emerge.

In projects with national governments and education providers we developed scenarios to assist Ministers and University presidents decide how and what they should teach in a world where automation and robotics may take away 40% of current jobs (Inayatullah, 2020). The first future is a world wherein educational systems continued to teach for jobs that no longer existed. The second future is where marginal change occurs. Small changes are considered such as teaching STEM or English or Mandarin, but the nature of teaching - rigid, at one campus with some virtual, some professor-based - does not really change. A third future, the adaptive, suggests that emerging industries needed to be analyzed and teaching needs to focus on them, i.e., 3D printing in health; the internet of everything (place, people, and nature); robotics; personalized precision preventive medicine; and ageing. This was teaching and learning for the emergent future - a world where the robot was one's best friend forever. In the last future, the radical, the transformative, the nature of the world changes so much that no one quite feels at home. We teach and train for a world after jobs. It is not just the shift to industrial to digital pedagogy, but a shift in which the nature of work, compensation, and life purpose are challenged.

TEACHING AND LEARNING SCENARIOS

No Change	Marginal Change	Adaptive Change	Radical Change
Teaching and training for jobs that no longer exist.	Catching up through STEM. Pedagogy remains rigid.	Teaching and training for tomorrow's jobs. New modes of pedagogy are created.	Teaching and training for a world after jobs. Core assumptions around work and life purpose are rethought.

Alternative futures can help shift the mindset of decision-makers, meeting them where they are at, and moving them to where they can be. While there are numerous scenario-based methods, we have used the Change Progression approach with various projects with national governments (Government of Malaysia, 2018: pp. 58-66). This approach integrates how the external world is changing and what actions actors can undertake. Thus, it not only reduces external variation but enhances agency, as action steps can result. In the first, even as the external world changes, the organization/institution in question either prefers a no change future or is unable to manage change. This could be because the weight of history is too heavy or because the capabilities to change are not present. In the marginal change future, the external environment continues to change, however, given the reality of politics – bureaucracy and power - only a few policies are successfully implemented. In the third future, the external world continues to change, and the organization/institution adapts to the changing world – implementation and adaption policies succeed. The organization or institution anticipates the emerging future and plays a role in shaping it. In the final radical scenario, the organization leads the future, the rules of the game are reshaped. Thus, the scenario structure moves from no change to marginal change, to adaptive change and then finally to radical or transformative change.

With the government of Egypt and the United Nations in Egypt we took this approach and explored alternative futures of the manufacturing sector (Inayatullah, Jacobs, Rizk, 2020). The scenarios were developed with national and international experts. The descriptions below are derived from the published report.[4]

In the first future titled, "the Gap Expands", there is a loss in competitiveness of Egyptian manufacturing and drop in export earnings. The gap between Egypt and other emerging production sectors globally widens.

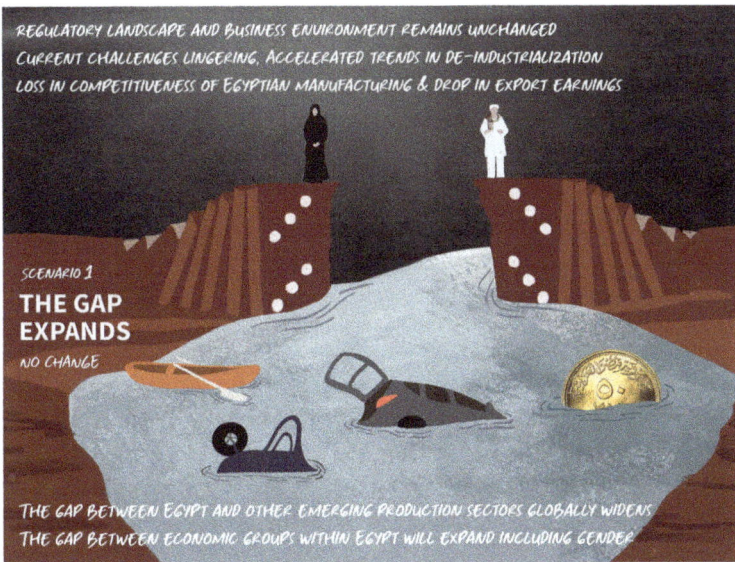

REGULATORY LANDSCAPE AND BUSINESS ENVIRONMENT REMAINS UNCHANGED
CURRENT CHALLENGES LINGERING, ACCELERATED TRENDS IN DE-INDUSTRIALIZATION
LOSS IN COMPETITIVENESS OF EGYPTIAN MANUFACTURING & DROP IN EXPORT EARNINGS

SCENARIO 1
**THE GAP
EXPANDS**
NO CHANGE

THE GAP BETWEEN EGYPT AND OTHER EMERGING PRODUCTION SECTORS GLOBALLY WIDENS
THE GAP BETWEEN ECONOMIC GROUPS WITHIN EGYPT WILL EXPAND INCLUDING GENDER

Illustration by: Charmaine Sevil

In the marginal change future, titled "100 million to a billion," there is a renewed focus on domestic and regional demand. The government removes institutional barriers and frees the economy.

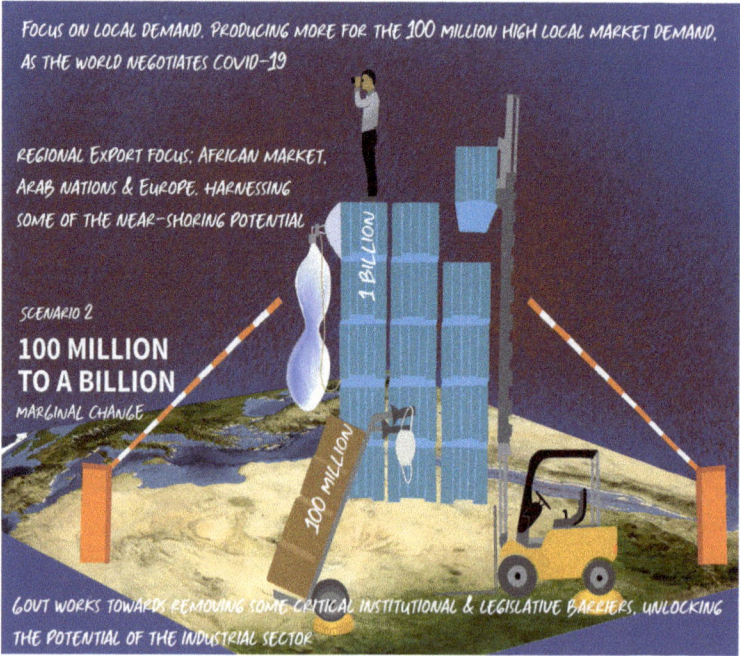

Illustration by: Charmaine Sevil

" Alternative futures can help shift the mindset of decision-makers, meeting them where they are at, and moving them to where they can be. "

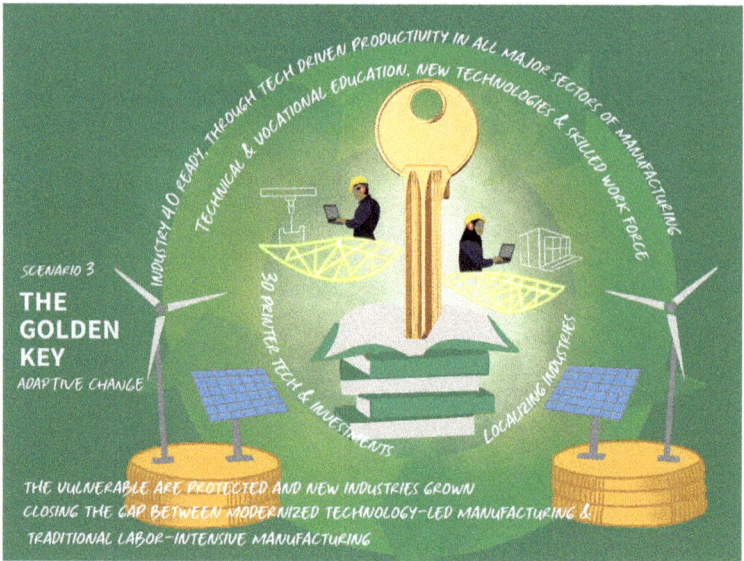

Illustration by: Charmaine Sevil

In the adaptive future, titled, "the Golden Key", manufacturing growth is created through protecting the vulnerable. The gap between traditional labor-intensive manufacturing and modern technology-led manufacturing is closed through education, internet infrastructure development, and localizing key industries through the use of 3D printing technologies.

In the marginal change future, titled "100 million to a billion," there is a renewed focus on domestic and regional demand. The government removes institutional barriers and frees the economy.

The radical scenario was called "Alibaba Transformation". In this future, the latent business potential of informal sector, smaller formal sector firms and youth bulge is unleashed through the linking of two areas: the informal sector (including micro-small formal enterprises) and digital platform technologies. The informal and education sector lead in the transformation of manufacturing. The informal sector, youth, and digitalization harness the vision of the future and technology to create breakthrough after breakthrough.

From these futures, a preferred future was articulated as well as strategies and recommendations going forward.

However, alternative futures thinking is also a way of being. One public sector leader informed me that when he negotiated with head of garbage collection in his nation, this approach was foundational to his success. He wished to convince the director to adopt driverless trucks. He refused, arguing they did not wish to eliminate their workers. "Our sanitation workers do more than pick up garbage, they connect with the community."[5] Most advisors would have left the discussion, but he remembered the core lesson of futures thinking - alternatives. He then asked, what about at night? Can we imagine a scenario where garbage trucks become driverless for night shifts? This led to a world's first of driverless garbage trucks.

Alternative futures thinking is also crucial in resolving conflicts. If those in conflict believe there is only one solution, one way to be, then the conflict is likely to continue. But if more and more scenarios are developed not only is it likely that the conflict will be resolved, but that the conflict will be resolved non-violently. More opportunities are possible (Hutchinson, 1996; Galtung, 1967; Milojević, 2008). One can move toward "our way" solutions instead of being stuck in "my way" or "their way" or "no way." In one workshop where there was conflict between preferred visions of the future city, the Green-eco city and the Glamour 24/7 city, both groups moved toward our way as they created common ground i.e. the Glamour city could not exist without the foundations of clean, green, pollution-free air. The green vision of the city needed ways to finance the future. Of course, as Milojević points out (2020), this is contextual, there are times when a no way approach is appropriate.

Scenarios also challenge the gendered nature of the future; that is, futures done well decolonizes power, allowing for agency to expand. They go beyond traditional technocratic forecasts of the future. As Milojević (2000, p. 895) writes: "Most woman futurists do not reject new technologies...but the focus is often rather on human relationships and more inclusive of the perspective of the powerless."

Scenarios for Milojević are important because they help "women develop strategies to try and avoid certain futures or at least diminish their impact. Scenarios also distance us from the present, creating alternatives that contest traditional gender roles (Milojević 2000, p. 895). "

Scenarios can be equally powerful at the personal level as well. Time given, I always try and develop personal scenarios. One community organizer articulated four futures of her life. The first was the integrated life, personal, family, and professional. The second was the opposite - the perfectionist, the need to make her life perfect and thus sabotaging integration. The third was life in stages - a time for the personal (marriage and children); a time for career; a time for social service. The final was her outlier scenario: running away to India to become a yogic nun. The scenarios clarified her life choices, allowing her as much as possible to be conscious about choices.

Another was focused on deciding the next phase in her career. She had to decide between continuing her career as an elementary school teacher in a non-supportive environment or take the risk and move overseas to join a doctoral program. Her first scenario was: "I'm coming doctorate" with the underlying metaphor of "happy but poor monk". The second scenario was the no change future, which she called, "Stay in Hell" with the underlying metaphor of "in the desert with one tree." In her third future, the doctorate was complete, and she was now back home. In this future, the underlying metaphor was: "normal person in a psychiatric hospital".

In her final scenario, she stays at the elementary school, accepts her condition. The metaphor was: "boiling frog." The scenarios helped her articulate what was most important to her, what she truly valued. After the scenarios, she realized it was not where she was at or which degree she had; rather, most important but the quality of her relationships, inner and outer. She called this the "sacred protective relationship." The vision for the future informed her choices.

Thus, as we move up the scale from social injustice (it is not fair), to risk mitigation, to creating alternatives, possibilities emerge and expand. The goal in this stage is to create alternatives, possibilities, to not become stuck on any one future, particularly any predicted future. This helps us move to the next stage.

> **Scenarios can be equally powerful at the personal level as well. Time given, I always try and develop personal scenarios.**

Directionality

Once alternative futures are explored, insights into the range of directions are gained. But which direction to go toward? This is next crucial part of the foresight process. Scenarios help clarify alternatives, but once there is clarity of costs and benefits, of desires and fears, there needs to be a decision as to what is next? We need to decide on a vision: where do we wish to go? Personally and professionally, where do we wish to be in a decade or two decades? The vision is crucial as it becomes the decisive indicator of what one should do in the present. Does a current decision align with where one individual or the institution wishes to be in a decade? Directionality is critical to harness personal and organizational energies. One corporate group asked for advice on the futures of cola. We provided our best insights into the risk of staying with a beverage that provided no measurable health benefits. Ultimately the CEO decided to focus on becoming the world's leading wellness company by 2035. From this vision, she began to move into the health industry. After seven years, over 50% of her revenues are now derived from health drinks and products (Cresswall, 2018).

Another group, a coroner's court, saw that the part of their work they believed the most significant and personally rewarding as justices was prevention not merely analyzing the factors that led to death. They began to imagine a future where they focused on well-being and prevention.

THE CORONERS COURT

Coroners Court 2030	Today	Preferred Future
Litany	Throughput. Recommendations	Reduced deaths Increased wellness Greater community satisfaction
Systemic	Paperbound Internally progressive: externally limited	Enhance efficiency through new technologies
Worldview	Paperbound Internally progressive: externally limited	Serve the community through proactive innovation
Myth/ Metaphor	Sprouting seed	Large blossoming tree

Using the CLA process of four levels of reality, they used what was working well in the present and magnified it, moving from a sprouting seed to a large blossoming tree. They did not wish to stop serving the community, but rather wished to enhance it through proactive innovation. However, they understood that many of their traditional administrative procedures needed to be streamlined so they could focus on what was of greatest value. To ensure they stayed on this pathway, they also changed their key performance indicators, the litany, what they talked about daily. In their preferred future, their guiding narrative would be the "large blossoming tree."

Visioning is more valuable when participants understand their zone of control - what they can influence and what they cannot. This allows for the vision to become reality. Cities are perfect examples of this. They have budgets and influence, but generally of the size where policy and strategy can make a difference. In numerous Australian cities, we have embarked on 2030 and 2040 projects (Russo, 2016). These worked well when we included three parties: citizens through foresight workshops; political, business, and community leaders through visioning and strategy sessions; and academics and research organizations to collect data on the past, emerging trends, and indicators of the desired future. In a recent city project, the past was used as an asset, to help set up the desired future. The refrigerator had been invented in the city and it was one of the first global cities to develop botanical gardens. The founding elders had created a public green space for future generations. Working with public officials, citizens, we developed a vision of the future. This was further narrowed down through a citizens' voting process to develop preferred trajectories. In another city, hundreds of vision ideas were collected. (Ding, 2005). These were then narrowed down to ideas that could be implemented. In all these processes, the vision and budget became linked; civic energy was enhanced through anticipatory democracy, and communities felt heard, even if no idea was implemented.

Ultimately, visioning is a victory of agency over structure, of what can be over what is.

In the earlier scenario case studies of manufacturing futures of Egypt, from the four scenarios, they developed their vision of the future. The preferred future was not just one of the scenarios but a higher order future, qualitatively different. In this future, a circular economy is created; the informal and micro firms lead in innovation; industry 4.0 is created giving young people a focus and hope; regional trade is dramatically expanded; social protection schemes are developed to ensure safety nets; near-shoring emerges, and most importantly, the economy is unlocked.

PREFERRED
FUTURE

PRODUCTIVITY ENHANCEMENT & GRADUATING A LARGE PROPORTION OF SMALLER INTO MEDIUM-SIZED FIRMS INTEGRATED INTO GLOBAL VALUE CHAINS
CIRCULAR ECONOMY MODEL IS REALIZED · INTEGRATION OF THE INFORMAL SECTOR & MICRO-SMALLER FIRMS & THE ECONOMY

THE ECONOMY IS UNLOCKED & BUSINESS ENVIRONMENT SEES SIGNIFICANT IMPROVEMENT
ACCELERATED TRANSITION TOWARDS INDUSTRY 4.0, HARNESSING A SKILLED YOUNG WORK FORCE

Illustration by: Charmaine Sevil

While some groups look at multiple variables in creating the new desired future, others hone down on the variable that can create the greatest impact, that can create the change. For example, a leadership group in Cambodia focused on moving from gender as linked to production to gender as empowerment. The present was essentially about how many shirts per day a woman garment worker could produce. However, in their preferred future, the vision, far more important was the number of women in leadership: in corporate boards, and as members in Parliament. They argued that this would not only empower but reduce risk, since data suggests that woman financial managers not only reduce investment risk but enhance profitability (Basak and Green, 2019).

> **"While some groups look at multiple variables in creating the new desired future, others hone down on the variable that can create the greatest impact, that can create the change."**

The following CLA shows their approach (Inayatullah, Durrani-Jamal, and Sandhu, 2020)

CAMBODIA CLA ON WOMEN AND LEADERSHIP

CLA	Current reality, 2019	Transformed, 2030
Litany	How many shirts produced per day?	Number of women in leadership
System	More mechanical work, everyone does the same work and a lot of rules to follow	• More thinking related work • More diverse work opportunities • More empowerment
Worldview	Rule-based culture with low status and low paid jobs – the Industrial economy	• Modern, greater use of technology, learning and exchange experiences, local and international, young and old – the Knowledge economy
Myth/ Metaphor	Garment worker = a woman	Leader = a woman

The implications if their vision became reality included: more women-oriented policies leading to increased women's income, less violence against women, new positive role models for young girls, and a growing income. However, they also understood that the male backlash scenario was possible, and thus they needed to not just increase the role of women in leadership but ensure men did not feel excluded as the pie increased. The vision of these Cambodian leaders was not to reverse gender hierarchy but to create a partnership society.

A global driver for a partnership society is the rise of the cultural creatives. This demographic group is focused on ecological sustainability, social inclusion, corporate social responsibility, and spiritual practice. They envision an alternative global future. At the heart of this new vision, argues Paul Ray (2002), are the values of women coming into the public domain globally for the first time in history.

Wellbeing is critical not just with cultural creatives. In a series of workshops with Brisbane Grammar School, indeed, in the preferred future wellbeing for all stakeholders: students, parents, teachers, the school adminivstration, indeed, the planet became the central variable (Inayatullah, S. and Roper, Ed. 2020). Similarly, with the Government of New Zealand, wellbeing is not just a value but a vision of a desirable future. Indeed, along with scenarios, they are in the process of developing visions for key areas such as budget (Charlton, 2019) and infrastructure linked to the larger vision.[6]

Illustration by: Charmaine Sevil

Visioning is often interactive. One private Montessori school uses visioning regularly to help decide direction and budgets. The school has done this three times over the past fifteen years. Teachers, students, parents, the board are all included in this regular and iterative process. Once the vision is set then a strategic plan is written, and funding sought for implementation. The vision not just helps sets direction but creates a community spirit and enhanced futures literacy. Realizing the vision or aspects of it create a momentum.

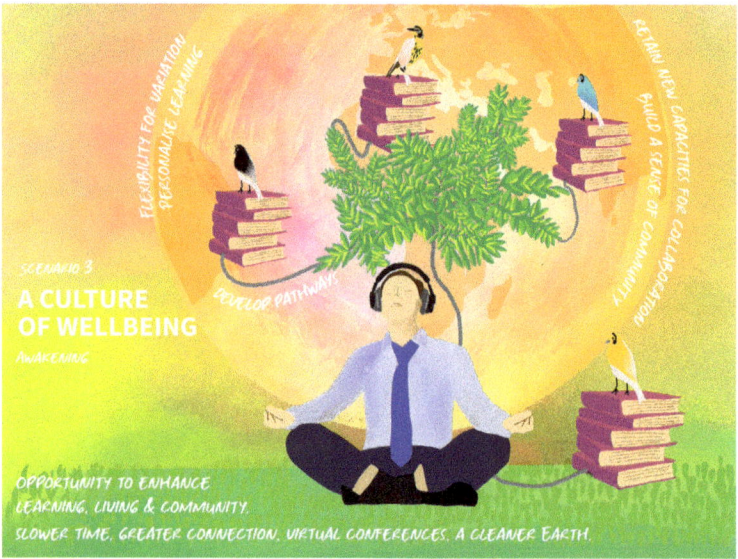

Illustration by: Charmaine Sevil

Making the vision real

Visions, however, without reality can reduce agency quickly. Visioning can be a direction, linked to the strategic plan. Visioning can be creative, highly personalized with the intent to imagine a different future. Visioning can also be fantasy, a way of avoiding what is painful, what needs to be understood and discarded. Visioning as such hurts the futures process.

Thus, to continue along the path of using the future to empower, we need to make the vision real, to allow the vision to enable and ennoble. Visioning is especially crucial for the structurally disadvantaged. In contrast to trend analysis, which takes the reality of the moving present - as evidenced with quantitative data - as defining, visioning is focused on the preferred. Trend Analysis, as Milojević (2000) writes, "offers no alternatives (...)while visioning in which the preferred future is developed and then the path toward it remembered is more relevant for women, and for other similarly disadvantaged members of global society."

To make the vision real, several processes help. Most significant are action learning, strategic plans, backcasting, and personal ownership of the future.

Action learning seeks to link the vision of the future with individuals using open space technology (Owen, 2008) to design projects and processes to create a difference. In one project on rural health futures, over 50 CEOs met to design a new health system. Over two days, they imagined the 5P health model (Cornell Tech, 2016). This image consists of moving toward: (1) Prevention (exercise, meditation, early check-ups); (2) Precision/personalized medicine; (3) Predictive health; (4) Participation (patients designing their health journey); and (5) Partnership (all agencies working together). Done well, this vision would dramatically reduce costs. It would do so by focusing on individuals in the context of their communities, use advanced genomics medicine to tailor health solutions for the individual, predict an individual's health pathway, work with patients so they could participate in their health decisions, and create health systems that work in partnership with each other. This challenges the generic, silo-based, problem-solving hospital health model. While the vision was brilliant, there was concern that this was too far in the future. How could we move forward? Using open space technology, ten working groups were created. Group leaders pitched the project ideas they wished to embark on. Of those ten, there were no takers for three of them. Seven groups developed proposals for next steps, such as developing a home-hospital, articulating system wide measurements for prevention, creating a one-stop health center, and so on. The director of health funded all seven projects. This created a quick planning cycle from vision to creation.

Of course, open space is not appropriate for every project. With a large professional group, Optometry Australia (2018), the vision was made real by participatory scenario planning, not open space. Foresight workshops were run for optometrists throughout the nation. This process led to considerable buy-in. During the national planning day, optometrists articulated a range of activities and steps they asked the national body to initiate. This was the case for the Hawaii Judiciary as well. There, after a decade of futures activities - primarily focused on emerging issues analysis - a national conference articulated core strategic recommendations to the Chief Justice (Inayatullah, 1991b). As there was deep inclusion of system actors in the process, it was relatively easy to gain legislative and executive approval for the changes.

Communify, an Australian community organization supporting the most vulnerable, has used futures every five years to articulate its vision. The vision then is translated into the strategic plan, which the Board and the CEO then enact. Participants in the processes know that their work, while fun, is also productive; it will lead to change. The futures process is used since it is inclusive, takes a longer view of time, can identify risks and emergent opportunities, and as it is grounded in depth, it helps ensure that culture does not eat strategy for breakfast (Ross, 2015).[8]

The vision also becomes powerfully real through participatory backcasting. Developed as an analytic approach by John Robinson (1982) and as a participatory method by the feminist Quaker Elise Boulding (1995), in this process, the imagined future is accepted as the reality, for example, by 2030. The past then is remembered. I ask participants to remember what happened in 2028, 2025, 2020, and so forth. Individuals who offer suggestions then move to the spot on the floor reflecting distance from the year 2030. A timeline quickly forms. Individuals then move based on logic, i.e., if there is new legislation that occurred in 2025, then there needed to be a social movement around the legislation earlier. There needs to be research done as to its implications. Funding for these actions would have to have been sought much earlier in 2022. Backcasting takes the mystery of futures back to practical strategy. There are clear steps that need to be done and a logical and rational narrative of the process to create 2030 is developed. If individuals find they are unable to create the backcast, it is almost always that the 2030 is too soon for the vision, 2040 is needed, i.e., more time is required for implementation.

1.The chart below is a backcast done with governors of Armenia (Inayatullah, 2019). Their vision was focused on renewable energy, digital literacy, and educational transformation. Four actions/processes were critical.

2.Ensure zero tolerance for corruption – this would create a culture of trust, an enviable investment climate, and a virtuous cycle of prosperity.

3.Investment needed to be green and sustainable. For them, this meant reducing energy costs, increasing well-being, the health, of citizens, and creating innovation that could lead to more innovation.

4.Investments needed to use new AI supported technologies. While these disruptions would certainly lead to some unemployment in the short run, in the medium-to-long run, new industries and jobs would be created. These would be clean, green, and smart.

5.The centre of Armenia, Yerevan, needed to develop in conjunction with its regions, and development in Armenia, especially development that leapfrogged, would not be possible without open borders and peace with neighbours.

BACKCAST BY ARMENIAN PUBLIC SECTOR LEADERS

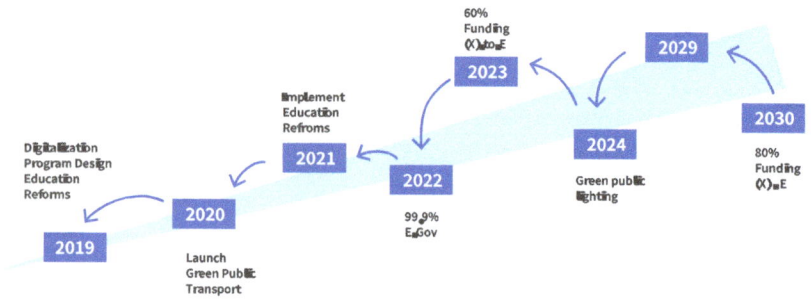

2019 — Digitalization Program Design Education Reforms

2020 — Launch Green Public Transport

2021 — Implement Education Refroms

2022 — 99.9% E-Gov

2023 — 60% Funding (X) to E

2024 — Green public lighting

2029

2030 — 80% Funding (X) = E

In our earlier example of the disability sector. Using backcasting, trajectory from the current problem of isolation to a new future of care connectivity was envisioned.[9]

Disability Futures Adrian Crothers:

2020: Investment

Regional aged care / disability clients have the technology and the confidence to organize all of their supports, able to select their staff according to similar needs and goals. Able to access their own medical appointments, banking, shopping, online appointments, online communities to target loneliness. Ability to maintain their own packages and 2 hour support live online from support coordinators carers.

2020: Social Isolation

Massive government funded rollout of technology and continuation of high speed internet coupled with a massive training campaign to ensure people and their carers are familiar with this new technology.

2030: Interactive care

Difficulty connecting, loneliness, lack of choice in support, difficulty accessing the basics, exorbitant, prices, lack of ability or access to technology.

As well, the future becomes more real - filled out - through the CLA process. This works as the preferred moves the abstract to reality. In the CLA process, the current reality is deconstructed at four levels. The first is the litany, the current measurement of reality, the current discourse. The system or the causative variables that create the litany are then debated. From there the underlying worldview or worldviews are mapped. Finally, the underlying metaphor that supports the entire narrative is discovered. From here, the preferred future is developed through articulating the new metaphor, the new worldview, the new system (technology, society, regulations), and the new litany, the new preferred measurement system. The following examples are of an educational school system from the view of students (Edmund Rice Education Australia, 2019).

CLA OF CATHOLIC EDUCATION

Catholic students in 2030	Today	Preferred Future
Litany	Mandatory schooling Standardized, outdated, restricted	Flexible, unrestricted, global Everyone has access Relevant and adaptable
Systemic	Segregated by status and gender. Restricted. Does not support individuality	Students control learning Increasing drive to learn Increasing access to education
Worldview	Recall and striving for results rather than knowledge	Knowledge is useful and adaptive
Myth/ Metaphor	Generic suit	Tailor-made suit

This next CLA was developed by Catholic church leaders in Australia on the futures of the Church.

CLA ON CATHOLIC IDENTITY

Catholic Identity in 2030	Current Reality	Transformed
Litany	Traditional, maintain Catholic identity for the good of faith	Transformational, gospel-based spirituality
Systemic	Faith is under challenge. Faith and the Church are losing relevance. There is a lack of alignment between the laity and the clergy.	Re-awaken the spiritual search where traditional categories have failed to satisfy
Worldview	One true faith	Community at the service of the world
Myth/ Metaphor	Fist	Open hand

While this works for large groups, making the vision real also can be enhanced through individual inner work. Individuals need to see themselves in that future. We often ask participants to write a day in their life in 2030. What are they doing? This definitional work again makes a vision, often vague for some, into something far more tangible.

The Metaphor

Once the vision starts to become real, we need to ensure that culture does not eat strategy for breakfast. In my experience here lies the power of story, particularly of metaphors that help support the new vision, personal or collective.

As developed elsewhere, we have argued that metaphor is decisive (Milojević and Inayatullah, 2015; Milojević and Inayatullah, 2021). "The metaphor," Spanish philosopher, José Ortega y Gasset (1925) once wrote, "is perhaps one of man's most fruitful potentialities (...) Its efficacy verges on magic." How one uses metaphor can define the results that are created, as argued by Thibodeau and Boroditsky (2011). As we know from many studies, if crime is described as a beast then there is greater likelihood of subjects arguing for jails and punishment. Presenting crime as a virus, then the intended policy result is more likely to be increased funding for education and poverty eradication. (Kelling, 1991). In the

USA, if one argues for welfare, then interest in the legislative bill drops dramatically (Stone, 2012). If one suggests charity for the poor, then it goes up. The welfare discourse creates the image of the person who does not work hard, indeed, games the system. The other of the innocent poor."

We have described this process extensively elsewhere (Milojević and Inayatullah, 2015; Inayatullah and Milojević, 2015) particularly in work on CLA. With one organization that sought to identify future risks, while there was intellectual excitement for this task, there was an uneasiness - would it be of any use, would decision makers find the information valuable, they pondered?

During the workshop, we realized that the current metaphor was a "toothless tiger". In this context, information about the future would only have an academic interest - which in policing means none at all. The toothless tiger story ensures no real actions can result. An alternative narrative that emerged as preferred was the guard dog. The guard dog is community friendly, and thus community engagement becomes a necessity. A guard dog has bite, i.e., it can protect citizens and hurt offenders if need be. But most significantly, the guard dog acts as an early warning system. Within this narrative frame, information about he future now can be sensible, of tangible use. Foresight suddenly not only makes rational sense, but it can also be a story that can make a difference (Inayatullah, 2018, p. 18).

Another large international organization desired to engage in futures activities but was cynical given that the scenario work they'd already done had not yielded enough "bang for their buck". They were surprised that when they sent foresight surveys for field operatives to fill out, there were few responses. The insight came in the narrative phase of the process. While there were a number of competing metaphors, the one that resonated the most with the seventy or so participants was that of an old, blind, crippled elephant. However, one scientist commented, "the elephant is already dead: we are too busy filling out reports to notice". Although the leading international organization on the topic, a division of the UN, it had failed to adjust to the changing world. When asked what type of organization they should become, what was an appropriate metaphor, the best response was: "We need to be like an Octopus. Our tentacles and brains should be everywhere. We need to become smart, swift, adaptable, and develop the ability to productively engage globally, everywhere." However, the elephant was dominant. The Centre was calling the shots and the shift to decentralized intelligence as exemplified by the Octopus may be a narrative too far.

Thus, finding the right metaphor and linking it to strategy and how we measure the future we wish for is critical. In a project for the People's Republic of China on educational futures, the sticking points, participants believed were four-fold (Asian Development Bank, 2020). First was the litany, the institutional control of all education. Second was the system of compulsory, age-based, place-based education. Third was the Asian worldview that education leads to a job, which leads to a successful life. And finally, in the China case was the metaphor of the dragon contained by the Great Wall. After exploring alternative futures of education, business as usual, minor reforms, and radical changes, they articulated their preferred future. This was a new litany that allowed for multiple choices. The underlying system would offer multiple pathways for students. Education would be less about a job and more about learning tools that led to self-mastery, global-mastery and about creating alternative and desired futures. The underlying metaphor was the dragon pulling China to globalization. The Ministry would thus create more flexibility and adaptability. The great wall was the story of the past. In the transformed narrative, the dragon flies above the wall, seeing the planet and helping citizens gain new skills not just as workers but as learners.

> "Thus, finding the right metaphor and linking it to strategy and how we measure the future we wish for is critical."

CLA ON EDUCATION IN THE PEOPLE'S REPUBLIC OF CHINA

The People's Republic of China	Current Reality	Transformed by 2030
Litany	Institutionalized school education	Multiple and varied approaches to teaching and learning
Systemic	Compulsory education with passive students	Flexible and diversified pathways with students incentivized to be active
Worldview	Good education leads to a good job and a successful life	Learning tools about self, the world, and the future is a measure of a successful life
Myth/Metaphor	The dragon bounded by the great wall	The dragon pulls China to globalized education

The metaphor must be linked to systems and strategies or it becomes empty words. In this project for a southeast Asian nation, participants envisioned moving from a leader in obesity to a leader in regional health. They then linked their new metaphor (eat to live) with taxation strategies. They wished to increase the cost of sugar and rice and reduce the costs of a plant-based diet.

CLA ON INDICATORS AND HEALTH
– SOUTHEAST ASIAN NATION

Southeast Asian Nation	Today	2038
Litany	The second most obese nation in the region	A regional leader in health indicators
Systemic	High standard of living with plentiful food. Subsidized rice. A sedentary lifestyle.	Taxation on sugar and oil, and a reduction of rice subsidies. Incentives to grow one's own food. A shift toward a plant-based diet and a reduction of meat eating. Incentives to encourage natural and organic foods.
Worldview	Rice culture	A health-centric culture
Myth/ Metaphor	Live to eat	Eat to live

Connecting story to strategy can be part of an overall systemic shift; or in this case, a design and building project. In work with a state-level deaf association, the CEO, Brett Casey, first embarked on a challenging narrative shift. He shifted the metaphor from losing one's hearing to gaining deafness. He wished participants in a CEO leadership futures course to see hearing loss as a positive, as a possibility to expand community and culture. From this course, he then presented these ideas to his Board, with the intent to create an integrated community with hearing and deaf in partnership. Phase one in this process is to create a deaf center of excellence. The next phase is to expand this center to an integrated community. Concomitant to this process as to expand the use of technology in providing services to the deaf community.[10]

Narratives and metaphors help us transform past, present, and futures not just at organizational and institutional levels but at the civilizational. Milojević and Izgarjan reconstruct traditional Serbian and European literature by changing the storylines and endings. As they write (Milojević and Inayatullah, 2015: p. 156): *endings are transformed so that instead of the girl being killed or walled, for example, she finds her freedom, or instead of the prince saving her, she finds her own salvation, or success is created through the mutuality of a community. In these stories, the beginnings may be the same, but as we move through conflicts, as we move through time, the endings change. The future is transformed through the exploration of alternative possibilities and a new conclusion and through the exploration of alternative possibilities.*

The CLA process focused on narrative challenges conventional categories. It uses depth as an asset. For example, in deconstructing the death of George Floyd, we go beyond the obvious (Inayatullah, 2020b). At the superficial litany level, it was the police officer, but really his ability to act was based on a system of policing where harming African-American males has become normalized. At this systemic level we query the training of law officers, we search for the level of infiltration by far-right domestic terrorists, we ask about the level of diversity training. Thus, at the systemic level, the cause of Floyd's death is not the individual policeman but the current system of law enforcement. If we go deeper to the worldview level, then the issue is spatiality, the division of American cities by race. We see the worldview of white fear of black men and historical and social injustice. Finally, at the metaphor level, certainly the main story is "I can't breathe". We then ask, what would a different world look like? The new litany would be Floyd is a respected citizen. The system is one of diversity, with rules that are not discriminatory. The worldview shifts to inclusion. The new metaphor could be "Black Lives Matter". As we move toward a third horizon, the long term, we begin to imagine a partnership society, where all consciousness, human and nature, matters. But first we need to address inequity, then move toward greater awareness.

WHO KILLED GEORGE FLOYD?

CLA	DECONSTRUCTION	RECON-STRUCTION
Litany	A police officer killed George Floyd	George Floyd as an exemplary citizen
Systemic	Discriminatory training, infiltration by extremists, and poor representation	Diversity training, Reparations, Black to black business
Worldview	Spatial exclusion	Economic and cultural inclusion
Myth/Metaphor	I can't breathe	Black Lives Matter

Metaphors thus challenge colonized pasts. This is so at collective and personal levels. One extraordinarily successful Asian executive woman who participated in a futures workshop writes:

I did not realize that I had a metaphor of myself that bounded me to my self-limiting litanies. The metaphor is that I am Little Red Riding Hood (a Western tale) who is given strict orders by her mother to go visit grandmother (family duties and obligations). And Little Red Riding Hood has to cross a forest to reach grandmother's house, and the forest represents the external world full I did not realize that I had a metaphor of myself that bounded me to my self-limiting litanies. The metaphor is that I am Little Red Riding Hood (a Western tale) who is given strict orders by her mother to go visit grandmother (family duties and obligations). And Little Red Riding Hood has to cross a forest to reach grandmother's house, and the forest represents the external world full of dangerous beasts and hidden dangers. Little Red Riding Hood is a powerless girl with no experience in the external world and she has to walk alone through this dark and dangerous forest. She's scared that she will not make it to Grandmother's house.

The new metaphor that works better for the adult self is that I am now Mulan, who has shown bravery for my clan and family. I fought the war and won and now, I am recognized by my peers, despite being a woman, that I have the capacity, the courage and determination to win. And, just like Mulan in the story, along the way, I found my own Captain who is by my side and we ride Mushu (the dragon's name in Mulan) together among the clouds ready to face new adventures together. I am no longer alone in my journey.

The beauty of this metaphor is that is no longer a Western-inspired tale, but an Asian one, which helps to get rid of the clash in cultural values. I also like the new metaphor because it is totally empowering.

This story, as with many others, moves from a narrative that limits power to one that enhances agency.

The metaphor is decisive in setting direction, creating the new. The metaphor process is of use for groups and for individuals. With individuals, as was the case in the above example of the transformation from "Little Red Riding Hood" to "Mulan" the CLA of the self process is used. We move from the litany of the problem, for example, "I don't like where I work", to the systemic causes, such as "they pay well but I have little impact." From systemic issues we shift to the worldview, that is, what are the origins of this challenge? Does this challenge feel like any other life challenge? It could be feeling stuck in a previous job or issues in youth. In this real example, the senior economist of an International Bank said his metaphor was "golden handcuffs." He earned well but felt trapped. Once the old metaphor is discovered then a new one is created. In this case, it was the "Midas touch." From the metaphor the new strategy is created. For him, this meant not just giving financial advice, but leaving the bank and developing his own skills in the market or creating a portfolio career.

In another case, a young detective said his current metaphor was "an Iphone in a room full of Nokias." As he was in a hierarchical police system, his views were not heard even though he believed he had the talent and novel skill sets. His litany was not fitting in, believing himself to be better. The worldview was created earlier in his life in school. In the transformed narrative, the story shifted to the "co-designed chip-maker." In this story, he was no longer passive but active. Hierarchy was transplanted by partnership.

This process is not a one and done approach. It can be done over and over as more clarity of the desired future emerges. One young person in his twenties shifted from his life as a post-graduate student (on a treadmill) to search for work (being in a candy store). However, in his case, there were suddenly too many jobs available, too much candy. He thus changed his narrative and closed many of the doors at the store, he refocused the preferred future. However, as the future changed – the COVID-19 pandemic – he realized at issue was not the job search per se, but his lack of energy, the fatigue many of felt from the lockdown. He shifted his story again to the "eternal energy machine."

What we have noticed is that the metaphor that is not working is often static. The new metaphor is active, it is freeing, creating possibilities and solution based. One young professional described the goal his CEO had set out for him as akin to being handcuffed and sent to fight in a professional boxing match. His traditional and successful way of dealing with situations was to be like a river: to find a way without confronting authority. As he described his situation further, it became clear to him that he was now fronting a dam. Should he take a hammer and destroy the dam, or…? His conclusion was to rethink the dam with pressure valves, releasing water (stress, conflict, decisions) as needed be. He went from powerless to now having a new story and action steps that he could attempt with colleagues.

The goal thus is to transform through depth, to create a new organizational or personal life story, to move from what does not work, to what works.

The metaphor as in the next example below need not be a phrase but a drawing or other mode of representation.

As I did the brief personal CLA the unanswered question that I have struggled with most of my life is "How does one live fully when one feels unworthy?"

Second layer: The systemic perspective.

I am a transracial adoptee and my adopted parents never gave me the feeling I was unworthy, in fact quite the opposite. However, the core child within me constantly reminds me so. Through my successes and failures, what goes through my thoughts is that I must have done something from birth to 19 months so terrible as to make my existence worthless. Rationally, I can think myself out of this, but I often spin out of control and find myself metaphorically pushing myself violently down rabbit holes of doubt.

My tension lies between my internal and external world. My internal world is where that small child lives, the one who wants to be held, loved, and told how much she is worthy not for the things she has done but because she exists. However, the external world often sends mixed messages of what is considered worthy. I am not able to navigate it and I fall into rabbit holes.

Third layer: Discourse/worldview.

The world view that is connected is the systematic discrimination, working for predominantly white institutions that do not value diversity (or just offer lip service), but at the end of the day close the door. I make the choice to let these actors play a large role in how I value my worthiness. I also let society play a role in how I determine my worthiness. Recordings in my head fast forward, rewind, and play," You would be enough 'if' you did XYZ or 'when' you obtain As I did the brief personal CLA the unanswered question that I have struggled with most of my life is "How does one live fully when one feels unworthy?"

Fourth Level: Myth/metaphor.

My metaphor isn't really a metaphor, rather, it is a concrete action. I draw with my right hand but lately I have been drawing with my left hand. It is more unsteady, and I have to think harder as I attempt to draw a picture. The drawings are very childlike. When I did the guided meditation, I was launched into this picture of children smiling with uneven smiles, not perfect bodies, and yet filled with joy. When I was guided up to the 6th floor of the tree, the future person I met was my adopted mother, my real mother. Her face was not her present face it was when we met each other when I was 19 months old and she was in her late 20's. It is strange to meet someone as they were in the past in the future, but she handed me a letter that told me "You are loved." As I read, the note, I stopped listening to the guided directions and burst into tears. I immediately started to draw those children that I saw in the mediation when I was metaphorically jumping into 2030 future. The attached drawing is what I did in a matter of seconds with my left hand, non-dominant hand. I later watercolor painted it with my right hand.[11]

Illustration by: Staci B. Martin

The Mantra

However, the earlier process assumes that we know our future best, that our rational mind, the choosing self is wise. In the final stage, done exclusively with individuals, we move from the rational to the post-rational or the intuitive. Developed by the mystic, Dada Pranakrsnananda (2011, July 31) this process uses mantra - or the sound that transforms - to intuit the new metaphor (Inayatullah, 2002). Mantra becomes therapeutic, indeed, transformative, argues Dada.[12]   The mantra opens one up to a transformative future. For those who find the spiritual connotations of mantra problematic, they can, as one secular scientist did, simply say the words "breathe in, breathe out," over and over. The intention is not to choose a new narrative but create a space for well-being, an opening, to allow a new future to emerge.

In the case of our youthful detective, when he imagined his new metaphor and connected it to a sacred sound what emerged was not a reversion to the iPhone in a room full of Nokias or the co-designed chipmaker but instead a warm loving sun. The mantra went to a deeper part of where he was - in this case, he was now outside the hierarchy-partnership worldview. He had shifted to a different framework.

One CEO, a cancer survivor, wished to leave her husband. She felt he had not been supportive during her health ordeal. Moreover, she now wished to travel the world while he preferred watching television all day. They had two different visions of the future. In the inner CLA process, she noted that not all her selves were aligned. Her "dutiful wife" self-wanted to stay with him. Her explorer self-wished to see the world, having seen how precious life was. Her current metaphor was "living life in a straight-jacket." In the metaphor process, she saw herself departing in a Ferrari. However, as she visualized that, she noted her dutiful self was upset. As she sat quietly to reflect, a new image emerged. This was the open-door carriage. She was still to leave him, but the door to the carriage was wide open. She hoped he would join her. If not, she was set to go alone.

With one doctoral student who was unable to finish her PhD, in the rational part of the process, the metaphor shifted from "deer frozen by headlights" to "the keymaker." In this transition, instead of being stuck not writing - she was afraid to finish her PhD, as she did not believe she had the skills to get a job - she saw herself graduating and creating keys so that she could become a successful academic, wife, and mother. When she went to the mantra state, the deer frightened by headlights became a horse bolting from the farmhouse.

A leadership consultant used the process with these results. Her effort was to link her three passions: (1) leadership for all, the masses, (2) leadership for activists who wished to transform the world, not just optimize performance, and (3) leadership for women in science, technology, engineering and management. In the first, her metaphor was "behind the curtain". In the second, it was the "harbinger". In the third, it was the "mirror". These three strategies reflected her three selves as well. When she imagined these metaphors and connected them to mantra - the new metaphor was the "walking stick". For her, this was the "tool through which grace could flow". It was a tool she could use to support her three narrative strategies.

The mantra process integrates and creates a new story for the participant. The technical aspects of the process are quite simple. This can be done with a facilitator who guides one through the inner discovery process or privately. First, the CLA of the self process is undertaken. Then, using either the old or new metaphor, the participants listen to a sacred sound - a mantra contextual to his or her life experience. For those challenged by the notion of the sacred, then the sound of "breathe in, breathe out" can be used. Once metaphor and mantra are juxtaposed, a new image, a new metaphor can often emerge. This then becomes the pull of the future, the new way forward. We then seek to develop systemic suggestions to support the new story.

Recently with one Chief Financial officer, her metaphor underwent a transmutation from "Atlas holding the world up" to "a community circle." She understood this to mean that she was overly focused on her individualistic efforts to lead her team, based on her life story of coming from a disadvantaged community. When she juxtaposed the image of the metaphor with the sound of the mantra, the new image emerged. For her, this meant to change her leadership style from pushing her team to new challenges to working with them to create a different future.

The mantra process helps imagine creating a new future, an authentic future. It adds a feeling dimension to the rational act of creating alternative and preferred futures. It moves the participant to see and act differently in the present. This process can take time, however. One senior executive of a global beverage company was using foresight to help reduce the risks to their supply chain. In the mantra-metaphor process, he saw a different future for himself. Three years later, we had contact and he commented that he was now finally beginning to live the vision he had created for himself during the futures course.[13]

Another professional who participated at a six pillars futures workshops shared that the process helped her change the gendered power dynamics in her household. In the mantra process, her metaphor transformed from "bag lady on the street" to "la matrone de la maison". The process gave her the direction as well as the strength to assert her wishes and empowered her when working with other family members to reach mutually acceptable solutions.

Be the Future You Wish to See

The futures journey has an external and internal process. It certainly has stages and states, phases and realizations. In my experience, a woman or man or community experiencing injustice - it's not fair - would find visioning and metaphor interesting, but one of their core selves, core identities would ultimately not find it relevant. An external systemic shift to reduce unfairness is required or theories that suggest that is possible. Or it needs a narrowing of the grand vision to one's zone of control, otherwise visioning or scenarios would be fanciful, out-of-the-box thinking that leads nowhere.

Once there is some progress - the world is or is perceived as fairer - then they often wish to reduce risk to the new system they have created. Once risk is mitigated, there is a desire to grow, to enhance possibilities. As Dada Pranakrsnananda has suggested, "the mind wants more, indeed, more is the metaphor of the mind."[14] With this comes the need to explore alternative futures, to test each future for robustness, to get out of the single solution box. From here, we can empower using the preferred future. Communities and individuals believe they can create a desired future. They can imagine a world they wish to live in. The vision imagined, however, without a process to create the new reality can lead to despair, cynicism. Our task as futurists is then to help link the vision to the day-to-day. The vision can become meaningfully real - meaningful and powerful - through action learning, backcasting and the CLA process of external and internal change, of metaphor and system. However, as individuals and groups begin the task of system change, it is critical that the narrative also shifts, otherwise culture will eat strategy for breakfast. The narrative explains, gives insights, opens new worlds, makes the complicated complex, and allows the seeds of change to flourish. However, ultimately, the collective is but individuals. It is we that must change. We are the culture. Metaphor and mantra can play a crucial role in helping individuals become the future they wish to see.

Futures thinking can thus help us understand that while a castle surrounded by hungry wolves is often our current reality, it does not have to be. Anticipation done well can lead to emancipation.

The mind wants more, indeed, more is the metaphor of the mind.

— DADA PRANAKRSNANANDA

REFERENCES

Anandamurti, S.S. (Sarkar, P.R.) (1973). *Baba's Grace*, Denver: Ananda Marga Publications.

Asia Development Bank. (2020). *Futures thinking in Asia and the Pacific: Why Foresight Matters for Policymakers*. Manila: Asian Development Bank.

Australian Government. (2017). *Parks Australia Fact Sheet - Uluru-Kata Tjuta National Park*. Retrieved fromhttps://www.environment.gov.au/system/files/resources/abf7defb-4118-4247-bb47-2d2d8681b6a8/files/uktnp-a4factsheet-tjukurpa-small.pdf.

Basak, S. and Green, J. (2019, October 16). Female CFOs Brought in 1.8 trillion more than Male Peers. *Bloomberg*. Retrieved from https://www.bloomberg.com/news/articles/2019-10-16/female-cfos-brought-in-1-8-trillion-more-than-male-peers.

Boulding, E. and Boulding, K. (1995). *The Future: Images and Processes,* London: Sage.

Cammett, A. (2014). *Deadbeat Dads and Welfare Queens: How Metaphor Shapes Poverty Law*, 34B.C.J.L. & Soc. Just. Retrieved from https://lawdigitalcommons.bc.edu/jlsj/vol34/iss2/3.

Casey, B. (2018, May 3). *Presentation at Melbourne Business*

School. Retrieved from https://www.linkedin.com/in/brett-casey-87657a121/?originalSubdomain=au.

Charlton, E. (2019, May 30). New Zealand has unveiled its first 'well-being' budget. *We Forum* Retrieved from https://www.weforum.org/agenda/2019/05/new-zealand-is-publishing-its-first-well-being-budget/.

Chen, K. (2019). Transforming Environmental Values for a Younger Generation in Taiwan: A Participatory Action Approach to Curriculum Design, *Journal of Futures Studies*, 23(4): 79-96.

Cornell Tech (2016, November 18). *The 4 Ps of Health Tech*. Retrieved from https://tech.cornell.edu/news/the-4-ps-of-health-tech/.

Creswell, J. (2018, May 25). PepsiCo to Acquire the Fruit and Veggie Snack Maker Bare Foods, *The New York Times*. Retrieved from https://www.nytimes.com/2018/05/25/business/dealbook/pepsico-bare-foods.html.

Dator, J. (2002). Advancing Futures Studies: Futures Studies in Higher Education. Westport: Ct., Praeger 21st Century Series.

Dator, J. (2011). *Futures Studies, William Sims Bainbridge, ed., Leadership in Science and Technology.* Thousand Oaks, California: Sage Reference Series, 1 (Chapter Four): pp. 32-40. Retrieved from http://www.futures.hawaii.edu/

publications/futures-studies/DatorFuturesStudies.pdf.

Ding P. (2005). Envisioning Local Futures: The Evolution of Community Visioning as a Tool for Managing Change. *Journal of Futures Studies* ,9 (4): pp. 89-100.

Edmund Rice Education Australia (2019). *Edmund Rice Schools in 2030?* Edmund Rice Education Australia. Retrieved from https://www.erea.edu.au/news/article/2019/06/02/edmund-rice-schools-in-2030.

Eisler, R. (1997). *Dominator and Partnership Shifts*. In J. Galtung & S. Inayatullah (Eds.), Macrohistory and Macrohistorians: Perspectives on Individual, Social, and Civilizational Change. Westport: Ct. Praeger: pp. 141-151.

Eisler, R. (1987). *The Chalice and the Blade: Our history, our future*. San Francisco: Harper Collins Publishers.

Ferguson, D. and Colditz, I. (2019, July 11). What does the future hold for livestock production in Australia? *Beef Central.* Retrieved from https://www.beefcentral.com/news/what-does-the-future-hold-for-livestock-production-in-australia/.

Foucault, M. (1984). *The Foucault Reader*. Ed. Paul Rabinow. New York: Pantheon Books.

Galtung, J. (1967). *A Synthetic Approach to Peace Thinking.* Oslo: International Peace Research Institute. Retrieved from

https://www.transcend.org/files/Galtung_Book_unpub_
Theories_of_Peace_-_A_Synthetic_Approach_to_Peace_
Thinking_1967.pdf.

Galtung, J. and Inayatullah, S. (Eds.). (1997). *Macrohistory and Macrohistorians*. Westport: Ct. Praeger.

Government of Malaysia (2018). *Framing Malaysian Higher Education 4.0.* Putrajaya: Ministry of Higher Education.

Hancox, D. (2018, April 1). The unstoppable rise of veganism: how a fringe movement went mainstream. *The Guardian*. Retrieved from https://www.theguardian.com/lifeandstyle/2018/apr/01/vegans-are-coming-millennials-health-climate-change-animal-welfare. Accessed 13 July 2019.

Hicks, E. and J. (2004). *Ask and it is Given.* Carlsbad, California: Hay House.

Hoffman J. (2019). Imagining 2060: A Cross-Cultural Comparison of University Students' Perspectives, *Journal of Futures Studies*, 23 (4): pp. 63-78.

Hutchinson, F. (1996). *Educating beyond Violent Futures.* London: Routledge.

Inayatullah, S. (1990). Deconstructing and Reconstructing the Future. *Futures*, 22 (2): pp. 115-141.

Inayatullah, S. (1991b). Judicial Foresight in the Hawaii Judiciary. *Futures,* 23 (8): pp. 871-878.

Inayatullah, S. (1991a). Rethinking Science: P.R. Sarkar's Reconstruction of Science and Society. *IFDA*, 81: pp. 5-16.

Inayatullah, S. (2002). *Understanding Sarkar: The Indian Episteme, Macrohistory and Transformative Knowledge.* Leiden: Brill.

Inayatullah, S. (2008). Six Pillars: futures thinking for transformation. *Foresight*, 10 (1): pp. 4-21.

Inayatullah, S. (2013). Using Gaming to Understand the Patterns of the Future – The Sarkar Game in Action. *Journal of Futures Studies*, 18 (1): pp. 1-12.

Inayatullah, S. (2015). *What Works: Case Studies in the Practice of Foresight*, Tamsui: Tamkang University.

Inayatullah, S. (2018). Foresight in Challenging Environments. *Journal of Futures Studies*, 22 (4): pp. 15-24.

Inayatullah, S. (2019, May 9). From Ancient History to a Transformed Future: Can Armenia Leapfrog? *Journal of Futures Studies*. Retrieved from https://jfsdigital.org/2019/05/09/from-ancient-history-to-a-transformed-future-can-armenia-leapfrog/.

Inayatullah, S. (2020a). Scenarios for Teaching and Training: From Being Kodaked to Futures Literacy and Futures-Proofing. CSPS Strategy and *Policy Journal*, 8: pp. 33-50.

Inayatullah, S. (2020b). Who killed George Floyd? A Causal Layered Analysis. Retrieved from https://www.youtube.com/watch?v=JWwDmp1yY5A.

Inayatullah, S., and Milojević, I. (Eds.). (2015). *CLA 2.0: Transformative research in Theory and Practice.* Tamsui: Tamkang University.

Inayatullah, S., Durrani-Jamal, S., and Sandhu, S., (2020, May 12). Garment workers to Women leaders and the Wise E-Buddha: Cambodia 2050. *Journal of Futures Studies.* Retrieved from https://jfsdigital.org/2020/05/12/garment-workers-to-women-leaders-and-the-wise-e-buddha-cambodia-2050/

Inayatullah, S., and Roper, Ed., (2020, July 21). Letros Get Flexible: Brisbane Grammar School Navigates the COVID-19 Crisis. *Journal of Futures Studies.* Retrieved from https://jfsdigital.org/2020/07/21/brisbane-grammar-school/.

Inayatullah, S., Jacob, A., and Rizk, R., (2020, November 3). Alibaba and the Golden Key: Scenarios of Manufacturing futures in Egypt. *Journal of Futures Studies*. Retrieved from https://jfsdigital.org/2020/11/03/alibaba-and-the-golden-key/.

Kelling, G.L. (1991). Crime and metaphor: toward a new concept of policing, *City Journal Autumn*. Retrieved from http://www.city-journal.org/article01.php?aid=1577.

Kelly, P. (2008). *Towards Globo Sapiens: Transforming learners in higher education.* Rotterdam: Sense Publishers.

Khaldun, I. (1967). *The Muqaddimah.* (N. J. Dawood, Ed.) (Franz Rosenthal Translator). New Jersey: Princeton.

Lamb, C. (June 11, 2019). Perfect Day Launches Ice Cream Made from Cow-Free Milk, and We Tried It, *The Spoon*. Retrieved from https://thespoon.tech/perfect-day-launches-ice-cream-made-from-cow-free-milk-and-we-tried-it/.

MacGeorge, R. (2019). The Case of the Unemployed Power Station. *Journal of Futures Studies*. Retrieved from https://jfsdigital.org/2019/05/20/disrupted-infrastructure-the-case-of-the-unemployed-power-station/.

Maruyama, M. and Dator, J. (1971). *Human Futuristics*. Honolulu: Social Science Research Institute, University of Hawaii.

Miller, R. (2018). *Transforming the Future.* London: Routledge.

Milojević, I. (2000). *Future Studies in Kramarae, C. and Spender, D. Routledge International Encyclopedia of Women:* Global Women's Issues and Knowledge. New York: Routledge: p. 895.

Milojević, I. (2005). *Educational Futures: Dominant and contesting visions,* London: Routledge, 2005.

Milojević, I. (2008). Making peace: Kosovo/a and Serbia. *Journal of Futures Studies*, 13 (2): pp. 1-11.

Milojević, I. (2020, February 11). Who is right, Lyn or Pam? Using conflict resolution scenario methods to resolve an organizational conflict, *Journal of Futures Studies*. Retrieved from https://jfsdigital.org/2020/02/11/who-is-right-lyn-or-pam-using-conflict-resolution-scenario-methods-crsm-to-resolve-an-organisational-conflict/.

Milojević, I. and Inayatullah, S. (2018). From Skilling for New Futures to Empowering Individuals and Communities, *Journal of Futures Studies,* 22 (4): pp. 1-14.

Milojević, I. and Inayatullah, S. (2015). Narrative Foresight. *Futures*, 73: pp. 151–162.

Molitor, G. (2003). Molitor Forecasting Model: Key Dimensions for Plotting the Patterns of Change. *Journal of Futures Studies*, 8 (1): 61-72.

Molitor, G. (2004). *The Power to Change the World: The Art of Forecasting,* Potomac: MD, Public Policy Forecasting.

Optometry Australia. (2018). Optometry 2040: Taking Control of our Future. Retrieved from https://www.optometry.org.au/wp-content/uploads/Policy/Advocacy/optometry_2040_-_key_findings__priority_commitments.pdf

Ortega y Gasset, J. (1925). *The Dehumanization of Art and other essays on Art, Culture and Literature*. New Jersey: Princeton Classics. New Release 2019. Retrieved from https://www.goodreads.com/quotes/295735-the-metaphor-is-perhaps-the-most-fruitful-power-of-man.

Owen, H. (2008). *Open-Space Technology.* Oakland: Berret Koehler.

Pauw, I. et al (2018). Students' Ability to Envision Scenarios of Urban Futures. Journal of Futures Studies, 23 (2): 45-65.

Peters, A. (September 28, 2018). This startup lets villagers create mini power grids for their neighbors, Fast Company. Retrieved from https://www.fastcompany.com/90241777/this-startup-lets-villagers-create-mini-power-grids-for-their-neighbors.

Polak, F. (1973). *The Image of the future.* (E. Boulding, Trans.). London: Elsevier.

Pranakrsnananda D. (2011, July 31). *Let's have a Heart Circle!* Retrieved from http://dadaprana.com/heart-circle.html?i=1.

Ray, P. (2002). The New Political Compass. *Yes Magazine*, Retrieved from http://www.yesmagazine.org/pdf/NewPoliticalCompassV73.pdf.

Rohrbeck, R. and Kum, M. (2018). Corporate foresight and its impact on firm performance: a longitudinal analysis *Journal of Technological Forecasting and Social Change,* 129: 105-116.

Russo, C. (2016). From the Gold Coast to Geelong: how cities are shaping the visions of their futures, *The Conversation.* Retrieved from http://theconversation.com/from-the-gold-coast-to-geelong-how-cities-are-shaping-visions-of-their-futures-69055.

Russo, C. (2016). Mapping outcomes of four Queensland City Futures Initiatives, *Foresight,* 18 (6): 561-585.

Sardar, Z. (2010). The Namesake: Futures; futures studies; futurology; futuristic; foresight—What's in a name? *Futures,* 42 (3): 177-184.

Sarkar, P.R. (1984), *The Human Society.* Kolkata: AMPS.

Schultz W. (2017). Assembling a Futures / Foresight Toolkit. Retrieved from https://medium.com/@wendyinfutures/assembling-a-futures-foresight-toolkit-c55a956a3676.

Sheraz, U, Inayatullah, S, and Shah, A (2013). E-Health Futures in Bangladesh, *Foresight,* 15 (3): pp. 177-189.

Sorokin, P. (1957). *Social and Cultural Dynamics,* Boston: Porter Sargent.

Stone, D. (2012). *Policy Paradox*, W.W. New York: Norton and Company.

Sutherland, B. (2018, October 22). GE's $23 Billion Write down stems from a bad bet on fossil fuels, *Bloomberg Businessweek*. Retrieved from https://www.bloomberg.com/ news/articles/2018-10-22/ge-s-23-billion-writedown-stems-from-a-bad-bet-on-fossil-fuels.

Thibodeau, P.H. and Boroditsky, L. (2011). *Metaphors We Think With: The Role of Metaphor in Reasoning,* PLoS One, 6 (2), e16782 DOI: 10.1371/journal.pone.0016782.

Tibbs, H. (2011). Changing Cultural Values and the Transition to Sustainability. *Journal of Futures Studies,* 15 (3): pp. 13-32.

Toynbee, A. (1972). *The Study of History*, London: Oxford University Press.

Voros, J. (2003). A generic foresight process framework, *Foresight*, 5 (3): pp. 10-21.

NOTES

Anandamurti, S.S. (Sarkar, P.R.) (1973). Baba's Grace, Denver: Ananda Marga Publications.

Asia Development Bank. (2020). Futures thinking in Asia and the Pacific: Why Foresight Matters for Policymakers. Manila: Asian Development Bank.

Australian Government. (2017). Parks Australia Fact Sheet - Uluru-Kata Tjuta National Park. Retrieved fromhttps://www.environment.gov.au/system/files/resources/abf7defb-4118-4247-bb47-2d2d8681b6a8/files/uktnp-a4factsheet-tjukurpa-small.pdf.

Basak, S. and Green, J. (2019, October 16). Female CFOs Brought in 1.8 trillion more than Male Peers. Bloomberg. Retrieved from https://www.bloomberg.com/news/articles/2019-10-16/female-cfos-brought-in-1-8-trillion-more-than-male-peers.

Boulding, E. and Boulding, K. (1995). The Future: Images and Processes, London: Sage.

Cammett, A. (2014). Deadbeat Dads and Welfare Queens: How Metaphor Shapes Poverty Law, 34B.C.J.L. & Soc. Just. Retrieved from https://lawdigitalcommons.bc.edu/jlsj/vol34/iss2/3.

Casey, B. (2018, May 3). Presentation at Melbourne Business School. Retrieved from https://www.linkedin.com/in/brett-casey-87657a121/

www.ingramcontent.com/pod-product-compliance
Lightning Source LLC
Chambersburg PA
CBHW052013030426
42334CB00029BA/3205